BECOMING the ENCHANTRESS

A MAGICAL TRANSGENDER TALE

KRISTIN KOWALSKI FERRAGUT

ILLUSTRATED BY COLEY DOLMANCE FERRAGUT

Loving Healing Press
Ann Arbor, MI

Becoming the Enchantress: A Magical Transgender Tale
Copyright © 2021 by Kristin Kowalski Ferragut. All Rights Reserved.
Illustrated by Coley Dolmance Ferragut

Names: Ferragut, Kristin, 1969- author. | Ferragut, Coley, 2003-
  illustrator.
Title: Becoming the Enchantress : a magical transgender tale / Kristin
  Ferragut ; illustrated by Coley Ferragut.
Description: Ann Arbor, MI : Loving Healing Press, [2021] | Audience: Ages
  5-8 years. | Audience: Grades 2-3. | Summary: On Halloween, her
  children's acceptance and love gives the Enchantress the courage to
  magically transform from a Wizard into her true self.
Identifiers: LCCN 2021001036 (print) | LCCN 2021001037 (ebook) | ISBN
  9781615995622 (paperback) | ISBN 9781615995639 (hardcover) | ISBN
  9781615995646 (epub)
Subjects: CYAC: Transgender people--Fiction. | Family life--Fiction. |
  Magic--Fiction. | Halloween--Fiction. | Animals--Fiction. | Youth's art.
Classification: LCC PZ7.1.F4645 Be 2021 (print) | LCC PZ7.1.F4645 (ebook)
  | DDC [E]--dc23
LC record available at https://lccn.loc.gov/2021001036
LC ebook record available at https://lccn.loc.gov/2021001037

Published by
Loving Healing Press
5145 Pontiac Trail
Ann Arbor, MI 48105

www.LHPress.com
info@LHPress.com

Phone 888-761-6268
FAX 734-663-6861

Distributed by
Ingram (USA/CAN/AU), Betram's Books (UK/EU)

DEDICATION

For Ethan
a wonderful little boy
growing into a charming young man
with a heart so big it's a wonder it fits in this world.

Thank you for your support,
for making parenting such a pleasure
and filling your sister's life with gusto.

On Halloween night when the moon was full a powerful Wizard set out to take his children trick-or-treating. He smiled at their costumes, the Dragon and the Knight! They filled his heart with joy, but still the Wizard was wanting something.

He found his best cloak, silk as soft as a kitten and purple as raspberry ice cream. Wrapped in the cloak, standing between his Dragon and Knight, he declared, "We are ready! Candy awaits!"

"One last touch," the Wizard added before going through the wooden door. He removed his pointed hat, hung it on the coat rack and placed a simple ring of tiny white baby's breath flowers upon his head.

And with that, the three headed up the twisting paths that lead to the sidewalks of the village.

The sidewalks were busy with trick-or-treaters, parents, and dogs zig-zagging around puddles from the afternoon rains. It was difficult not to bump into people.

When his son almost stepped right into a little pug dog, the Wizard made the Knight go up in the air to float just over the now wildly barking puppy. Giggling, the Knight turned to the Wizard who winked. "Again, again!" the Knight begged.

"We'll see what other magic the night holds in store, son," the Wizard called back to him with a playful grin.

He soon made good on the promise, making decorations of hanging skeletons dance as the Knight and Dragon climbed the stone steps of the house at the corner. A chorus of children laughed, at least until the Wizard had a skeleton reach right into the Dragon's pillowcase and help himself to some candy.

"Hey! No fair!" the Dragon protested. The Wizard raised both hands with a bowing of his head, as if to say he would surrender his tricks.

In looking down, he caught his image in a puddle and liked what he saw. He often frowned in mirrors but now felt at home in his reflection. The Knight walked back to the Wizard and took his hand to lead him on.

"Excuse me ma'am," one lumberjack said, having accidentally knocked into the Wizard. The Knight went to correct the lumberjack, thinking, *He's a sir*, but seeing the Wizard's smile, bright as the stars, the Knight said nothing.

"Trick-or-treat!... Thank you!" While the Dragon and Knight racked up more and more candy, their pillow cases getting heavier and heavier and their legs getting tireder and tireder, the Wizard's smile grew brighter and brighter.

"Would you like some candy ma'am?... Your children are adorable, M'Lady... Such polite children! You must be one proud Mama..."

The Wizard beamed.

Eventually, the crowds thinned and porch lights went dark. "I'm tired, Dad, can we go home?" the young Knight asked.

"But it's such a wonderful night! Let's stay out for a spell longer."

The Knight sighed. There was no use arguing with the Wizard. The Dragon dragged her pillow case on the ground barely able to lift its weight. "Can we please go home now?" she asked the Wizard.

The Wizard found a tree stump in a quiet place and sat. The children snuggled up beside him. "I just don't want this night to end," he finally said.

"Is it the dark you want to keep?" questioned the Knight.

"No, I'm happy enough with the light of day."

"You want more candy?" asked the Dragon.

"I love watching you collect your treats, but no. I'd be glad to skip the candy."

"Then why won't you take us home?" asked the Knight pointedly.

"I want to stay in my costume," answered the Wizard slowly. The Knight and Dragon agreed that he could dress up whenever he wanted. That they could all wear their costumes the next day. The Wizard smiled at the children's kindness, but said wearily, "No, that won't quite do. I want to be my costume. No, that's not quite right."

The Wizard swallowed and took in a big gulp of air. "I think I am my costume. My pointy hat and day-to-day clothes, it's not really me. I want to switch my 'normal' self for my Halloween self, since this is the most like myself I've ever felt."

The Dragon and Knight studied him. He did look beautiful in his crown of flowers and soft, purple cloak. The Knight asked, "Would you then be a 'she' instead of a 'he'?"

"Why, yes! That's it!" The Wizard smiled at the Knight gently. "Do you understand?"

The children looked at each other. Of course they didn't understand. How could they understand? The Dragon understood that her costume itched and that she couldn't wait to change into pajamas. The Knight understood that his legs were sore. He wanted to sit down and eat some of his candy. But, looking at the Wizard, they did understand that he was happy.

So the Knight said, "Sure, be a 'she'. As long as you still take me out and play with me."

And the Dragon said, "You're a Wizard! You can make yourself whatever you want to be! Go for it!"

So the Wizard picked up the little Knight to piggyback him through the village, back to their home while the Dragon walked quickly by their side.

Once home the Knight sat upon the round, red rug, spreading his legs to the side and his candy out before him. The Dragon changed back to a young lady, put on soft flannel pajamas, and lay on the floor beside her brother. They both watched as the Wizard made the spell.

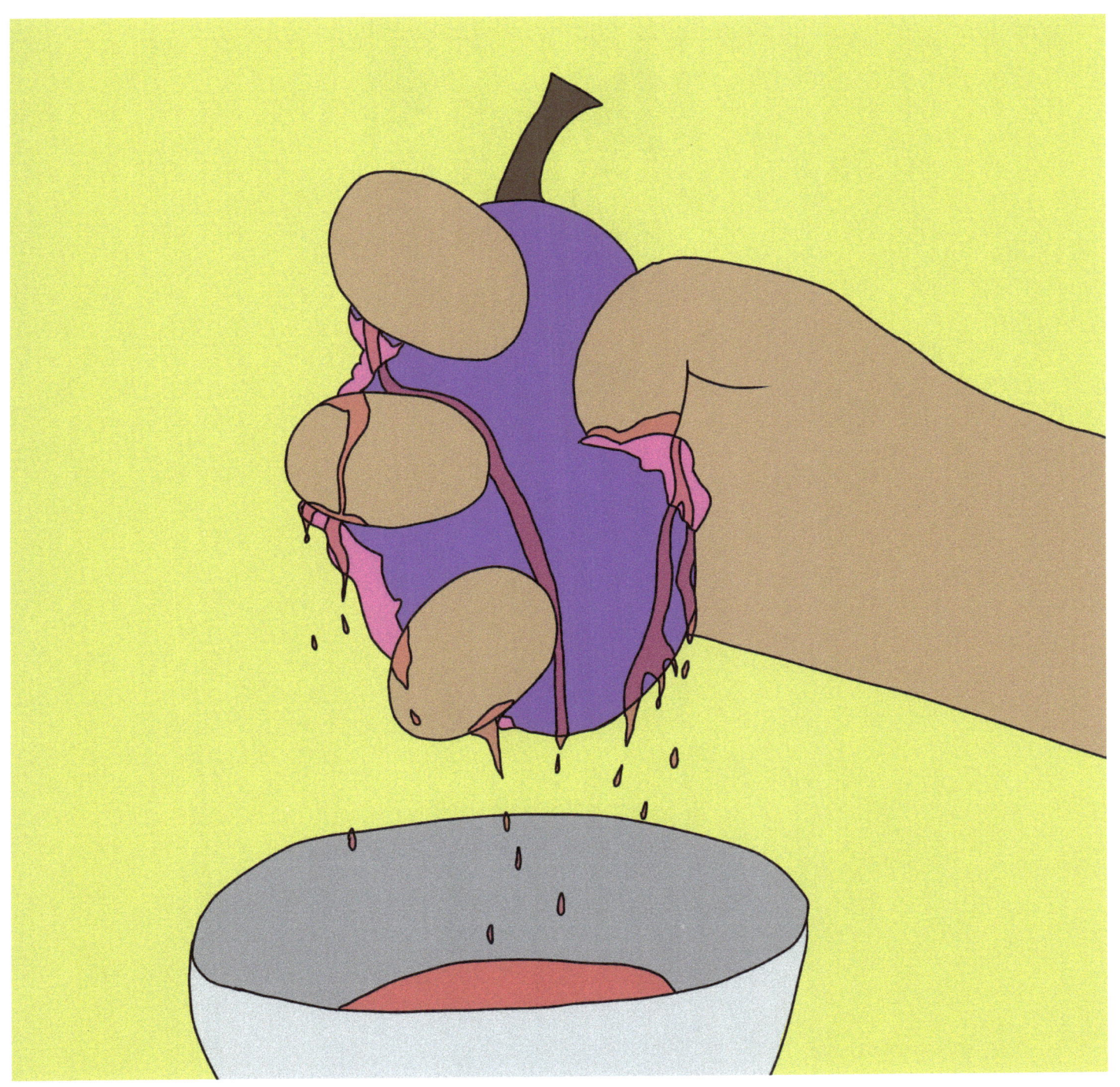

Removing his cloak and whispering magic words, the Wizard turned the fabric into ripe fruit that the Wizard crushed into a silver cup, and then drank.

The drink started out a bit sour, then turned sweet. It smelled like berries, honey, lemon and seaweed and fizzed in the Wizard's mouth, then warmed his throat. The children saw their beloved Wizard turn into a magnificent Enchantress.

The children rose from their place on the rug, being energized by magic in the room, and ran to hug the Enchantress who held the heart and soul of their beloved Wizard.

"You did it!" the girl exclaimed. "You became your costume. You're now a woman."

And the three hugged and laughed while the Enchantress wiped the berry juice from her upper lip and kissed her children, always so grateful for them.

For Parents and Guardians

A primary way children learn about the world is developing an understanding of categories: real/pretend, friend/stranger, boy/girl. Gender is one of the earliest categories introduced. Indeed a child's label of "mom" or "dad" for a parent is defined by gender. To shift understanding of these categories and labels may be confusing. It may even be difficult for a parent to find an entry point for such a discussion. This book was developed from a need to find that entry point.

I drafted this book to introduce transgender to a young boy. Attempts to discuss terms around gender – gender identity and transgender, went over his head or bored him and attempts to share videos of transgendered celebrities as an inroad to conversation were difficult for the boy to take seriously. A fun and gentle tool seemed necessary and ultimately this book served that purpose. After having the book read to him the boy exclaimed, "Hey, maybe the Wizard is like Dad!" The boy then changed the topic, going on a long wag about Pokemon. But a connection was made.

The peace that the boy made with having a transgender parent evolved over the next few months, never requiring an in-depth conversation. The variety of reactions that a child may have and the specifics of each situation are likely near-limitless. But I think there are some lessons learned within this book and within my experience that may be helpful in similar situations.

That I maintained an accepting and uplifting tone when discussing the boy's transgender parent modeled how I hoped the boy would respond and he took the prompt. It seemed important at least for this child that I did not force a conversation, but allowed him to think it through and raise the topic and ask questions when he felt comfortable to do so. When the boy did ask questions, I tried to convey the message that what *does not* change with gender roles or parents' marital status is the unconditional love of a parent for their child. While this book is a transgender tale, it is fundamentally about love and acceptance between a parent and her children.

Acknowledgements

From Coley:

To my amazing Enchantress Mom who inspired this book.

To Chris for offering feedback, suggestions, and support; letting me bounce ideas off of him, and being my rock.

To my close friend Jhanaijia who supported me through this process and always welcomed my sharing any and all creative ideas with her, even when it took hours.

To my Mom for inviting me to collaborate and for her all-encompassing appreciation of me and support of my creative work.

From Kristin:

I thank my insightful writer friends who offered valuable suggestions and feedback for this book, including Jay Hall Carpenter, Serena Agusto-Cox, and Cristina Hanif. I thank Tammie Snyder for her persistent encouragement that I seek publication. And a heart-felt thanks to my awesome daughter, Coley, who provided her vision and creativity as illustrator. I'm grateful every day for her talents and insights and for her sharing them with me and the world.

Finally, thank you to Loving Healing Press for publishing *Becoming the Enchantress* and offering direct and helpful instruction throughout the process, as well as for publishing so many other important and necessary books.

About the Author

Kristin Kowalski Ferragut is the author of the poetry collection *Escape Velocity* (Kelsay Books, 2021). She teaches, writes songs, poetry and prose, hikes, and participates in readings and workshops in Maryland, where she lives with her two creative, lively, and supportive children. Her work has appeared in *Beltway Quarterly, Fledgling Rag, Bourgeon, Mojave He[Art] Review, Anti-Heroin Chic,* and *Little Patuxent Review* among others. For more information, visit her website: www.kristinskiferragut.com

About the Illustrator

Coley Dolmance Ferragut is an animator, digital artist, and actor who investigates themes of class and social justice in her work. A high school senior, this is Coley's first published book.